BEST BONES

PITT POETRY SERIES

Ed Ochester, Editor

BEST BONES

SARAH ROSE NORDGREN

UNIVERSITY OF PITTSBURGH PRESS

Published by the University of Pittsburgh Press, Pittsburgh, Pa., 15260
Copyright © 2014, Sarah Rose Nordgren
Manufactured in the United States of America
Printed on acid-free paper
10 9 8 7 6 5 4 3 2 1

ISBN 13: 978-0-8229-6317-2
ISBN 10: 0-8229-6317-5

for my family

and in memory of Paul Linder Nordgren

(January 27, 1988)

I hear the weather

        through the house

    or is it breathing

        mother

         —Lorine Niedecker

CONTENTS

BEST BONES

FABLE

I pull myself from the water by my hair

Shake the leaves out of sleep

When garage-entombed at night

I perch on a child's bicycle

Wearing mother's nightgown

Frayed lace through winter

Growing back to perfection

I am the oldest daughter in the story

The one whose shoes floated downstream

Who baked bread in an underground oven

The dark jealous girl walking

Barefoot before the king

So far north now and west of Helsinki

I make my nest and lie in it

Run furrows with my fingers in cold so close

It doesn't feel like weather

1

STILL BIRTH

The wall should be strong enough to break
the force upon it. Wind tunnels
right up the street from the sea, battering
the glass, forcing itself through wooden
slats, and the pages of the book
flutter crazily. Content usually roots
story to ground, but I sense it
shivering around you when you turn
half-asleep in bed, disturbed. You wake
from the story I was telling like
the second half of the book fell
into the water when the binding
gave, replaced with the sound of rushing.
The introduction was too long, but
the invisible boy had already traveled
for a year and a day, had tamed
the wolf in the lightless forest, fought
the man with the giant red face, but
he had not yet bought the globe that
(he would discover) could take him anywhere,
not yet come upon the broken eggs
with pennies inside. Though you know
the story, I mean to remind you
he will, eventually, return. Not in body,
no, but every time I tell it he becomes
more real. This is one of the stories
we live in against nature—I was trying
to tell you over the wind. If you learn anything
from living in this house, it will be how
to survive a variety of interruptions.

TEMPORARY RIVER

When the streets flooded that summer
and our homes became distant shores
across the neighborhood, I had no boat,
just one cracked paddle from the shed,
spider-webbed. I loved you then,
before we wore shirts, carried wallets
and umbrellas, before we knew to worry
about the river moving through town,
thick with filth. The backyard was deep
and tomatoes sank to the bottom.
Like loose teeth, the carrots were pulled
from the garden. Our parents warned us
of the rusted cans and snakes.
But up to my knees on the patio, I saw us
mirrored in the surface: your thin arms
and wet hair; my dark eyes and bony shoulders.
Years after, our bodies divided
like a cloud the wind forced in two directions,
or the morning after a small town in Texas
slides from its foundations, I've never known
why I'm living this life and not another.

*the poison
of what might
have otherwise
been*

REMARKS ON THE MORNING'S WORK IN WINTER

One hour alone is worth two after your master
has risen. The streetlamps, bright

and silent in the snow, stalk
your private movements. Rise early,

for the mornings are shorter now, and perform
your dirtiest tasks first.

Scrub the hearth grates, followed by your own
body, with a stiff brush. Slippers
or light shoes will ensure you glide between

rooms like your grandfather's ghost.
You may be required to kindle

three or four fires before daybreak,
but their warmth is not for you.

Clean the forks in a keg of sand and straw
till they glint like teeth. Hold the lady's

white shoe in your hands like a living dove:
Caress it with egg whites and milk.

You may find that the quiet, as it bleeds
in through the window frames
and from beneath closed doors behind which

people lie dreaming, deceives you into
believing, for whole moments, that

you are a part of this home: That the space
on the floor where you kneel

polishing brass handles was exactly measured
for the width of your shoulders,

pelvis, and knees, the dark mahogany
of your skin blending perfectly with
the other furniture.

THE WIFE

When I became one
I gave over the most of me.

I was earthly delight:
a gift of cherries

in a wide wicker basket.
I felt, finally, necessary.

No one, save him,
could command my

movements, and
command he did.

Stepping to like a mare,
I was rewarded

according to my struggle.
I became more cre_turely

with each passing year.

9

THE MISTRESS

Half-sleeping, you brushed my hand off—
Wait. So in my dream your tie unknotted,
waistcoat with watch chain, English-cut suit
unraveling. My ribbons fluttered. Corset
wrenched open like a fowl's rib cage.
Wigs tipped as we backed into the pantry:
breath catching between the walls,
hiding from the party.
                              Was it silly to try and live
this way, kept woman ignoring her history,
speaking with stockings under a wooden table,
dust-covered? Maybe I wanted you
to pay me. Trade fur and fabric for hair
and skin. For you to buy costumes
for every character, and me to wear them.

A BATHING GOWN A GIRL CAN MAKE

A girl usually wears a costume. Plain blue is suitable
for tightly clinging knickers fastened on by buttons.
The part not shown in the picture slips in and out
of the front, which is slit. White bone buttons
are made firm to cut up the legs. If it is inconvenient
to machine the knickers, stitch for an inch or two
in position. If the girl understands anything,
it will not do to make the costume an ample room.

THE ONLY HOUSE IN THE NEIGHBORHOOD

The stove doesn't work. The food is painted
on the refrigerator door. No stairs join

the three levels, and the residents flit
between them: colorful, mute birds. Days

pass with the click of a switch and no matter
if Baby bathes with his clothes on, or Mother

in her fitted purple jacket, heeled shoes,
and with her wild silken hair spends a week

facedown on the laundry room floor, or
if when Father goes to work he is really only

waiting behind the sunroom to come back home.
There is a birthday party nearly every day,

no fear of death or failure, no mortgage
to pay, no money at all. And if the tiny pink

phone in the kitchen never rings, and the doors
don't open, and if the family can't bend

their knees to kneel in the warm square of light
on the plastic-wood floor, they still lie

ready for you to set the table, snap the garden
fence back into place, position the pink crib

next to the blue, fix the girl onto her rocking horse,
and let your hand push the thing until it topples.

THE LORD IS RISEN INDEED

Sun silences the house. Between bough
and twig, a splintered branch. Mother stands behind
the wall. It is miniature: the baby's coffin

floating rooms like a canoe at dawn, smudging
wood floors like water. I want so much to see
his face, eyelids blue and shining under lamplight,

but he is wordless, invisible. We paint Easter eggs
for him, the prince in the moving tomb,
and find them in the grass all blue and spotted, slick

with baby slugs. Before the service, I refuse to wear
my dress. Want to look older for the limo ride.
Mother is a silhouette coming downstairs.

The women have eaten fruit and drunk their coffee.
The sun rises over the lawn where forgotten
eggs hide. The Lord is risen indeed.

Lilies light the way to the humming car, full
of believers. I sit to the right of my father.
My cousin's dress is too big for me.

SISTERS

the duckling in the shoebox dying fluttered fast
its leaves and twigs I am green
transparent sister told my sister her legs are not
gorgeous crawling to the bathroom
said you both like that anorexic look but not me
on TV a wrestling match the mean
woman in leather tore up the drawing from that retard
who loved her once I pissed my pants
laughed too hard sat in the driveway for an hour
on the bus the drunk girl cried
I've just been through hell I'm supposed to be
a bridesmaid where is my dress
I've lost the two people the African Gray in summer
flew up into the trees from my father's
shoulder where are the two people that I love?

WHITE SHEEP. WHITE CLOUD.

A child went missing from our family
who made us whole. Left the room thin as paper:

white sheep, white cloud, white floor.
The way our Mother waited you would think

she hung from a string upstairs
while Dad sang rhymes straight out of his head

making us piss ourselves giggling.
We knew someday we'd be mothers too

loving the still babies inside of us.
All spring we searched for eggs in the yard and fed

ourselves from the freezer. Walking barefoot
through the house, we never touched the white-

hot handle. Mom, Dad, tell us how
we could have taken care of you much better.

GENTLE DOCTOR

Doctor Seismograph, who records
the movements of the earth,
learns what we cannot.
He listens through his stethoscope
first here, then a little to the left.
Feeling the contractions, each
vital swing, he scribbles them down
so we can read them.

Only the gentle Doctor knows
what life is like under the black crust.
Do his instruments possess
more intelligence than us? We wish
him to remain here long enough
to attend the delivery day, but
what will be born of this
business the Doctor refuses to say.

1917

The holiest thing a mother does is know
your name long after her skin

disintegrates. I stand in a dark room imagining
my birth in 1917, so I can reverse

each injury her body takes. If history
were a computer programed by a genius child

on the best day of his life, her guts would be
tethered to her spine more tightly.

When she hunched over the steaming
kitchen sink, it would be yellow petals pouring

from her eyes. Her breasts would ungrow
to fresh mosquito bites, and the tiny,

plastic Reset button, installed
in her chest so carefully, would glow.

2

EXHUMATION .

I am the woman lying on her side across the van seat,
wearing a gray face, apparitional through greasy

windows as you walk past the railroad ditch
early morning on a whim, wanting to watch the sun

rise like you haven't in years. My life is under yours: in-
consolable, bathed in drainage, a midden of cracked

bottles, swollen tampons, rusted metal sheets cast
from the clamor. You flasher of future, your liver and lung

are fleshier, pinker. When they excavate me they will find
my many napkin writings, twenty rooms I built

from twine, dictionary of waste in which I define
your failure. Meanwhile: I'll retire to my atrium, washing

my perpetually warm body, liquid touching liquid
as it cools. The pipes are beginning to freeze. The all-night

factory shuts down at five. When the lights die you
disappear into a wooden structure and wonder

what you've done. Even if you'd brought your camera,
you couldn't click me. My face is an aluminum dish.

MY GRANDMOTHER'S BELONGINGS

Everything so organized, so fragile.
I look into objects now to please me,
smile to the silken face I wear
tonight, which is yours. The tiny boxes
hold northern air, eastern air
you saved in a box, particles
of spice and clay. Silk stockings
to put on with gloves. I wear you
when you were eighteen and delicate
as a scarf and I put you on
delicately. You don't mind me, do you,
combing the threads out, smoothing
your fingers, a student
gathering evidence, pushing
into the quiet like you must have done?

MARY

There was a hypothetical pregnancy.
The woman in question accumulated a box full
of video cassettes featuring pregnant
characters. She wore beads around her waist
and sat up late in bed with a shawl
of her own hair. Roommates circled
her like roosters, offering her most tender
bites of meat, and the apartment
reeked of sweat and powder. And because
in the end there was no fetus
she got to live for several years like this,
long-awaiting. And because I was only
a visitor, I envied the attention paid to her
by God, how He doted on her body.

TO MY DAUGHTER

Nov. 4:   I find you hidden under decomposing
            leaves, curled cold like a sleeping grub.
            I touch your face egg-white
            but smudged with crumbling earth.

Nov. 5:   You scream tattered moths as I lift you
            from your crib. Your winged
            voice flutters my cheek, then flies
            wildly around the room.

Nov. 27:   The Civil War. Hearing your shouts
            from a burning tree, I watch your arms
            wrapped tight around the body
            of the hickory, like a chased cat.

Dec. 1:   A terrible light pierces the windows;
            the eye altering alters all. Looking back,
            you are an eaten peach, your flesh
            cut off roughly from the center.

Dec. 9:   My body bulges with your pulsing
            weight. Outside, ice. I spit out a silver key
            and try it in my wooden navel. Opening,
            I extract your tiny, ticking heart.

SURROGATE

My friend gives me her gray slip
of an infant to hold in my belly.
He is not ready: limp slinky, back-
bending out of my hand
repeatedly. He must go back into the dark;
so I am honored, I am
lonely. I work slowly, absently,
chewing on tokens instead
of real money. I feed other people's
children through tubes,
filling them gradually like little
swimming pools. But I am
the receptacle: the other mind—
I wait to feel wanted and used. Take
what others don't have
time for: white, bothersome grubs
curled downward in the yard.
If never desired by men, then I'm loved
by those half-formed figures
who arrive, sterile-plattered,
to fill that ravenous maw.

INSTRUCTIONS FOR MARRIAGE
BY CAPTURE

Crinolined, I mime distress.
Flesh crimped. Mouth

ready to un-mussel. To open
the shell the knife must be

straight, and to hell
with alectryomancy, your cock

deciding which kernel comes
easiest to the beak.

This is survival of the bold:
to fling the child over

the shoulder and proceed
uninvited through her door.

I am shamed into shaking
my tail, and so it is

I tear willingly. Make no
error: I had a choice

but when it happened
I wept, saw blood sewing

a fine lace across
the mud. No witch can shed

more than three tears,
and those from the left eye

only, so be sure my real
face is under here.

WALLFLOWER

There's this girl the whole world loves
for the ratio she paints against the sheets.

Her skin is stained darker than mine so
I envy her, also the way

she stares in my direction, brainless
as a finch. With the cameras

rolling I'm careful to speak my lines plainly, cup
the tendril of her in my hand

like a broken bracelet chain. But between
takes, I become a thief.

Naked, I have no pockets or sleeves, so
I horde what little bits of her I can

in my cheeks. Sometimes I tell her
I'm a man so she'll trust my compliments,

ease near to me over the steam rising
from a flock of Styrofoam cups. Then

it's simple to reach inside her, lighting
the white wick so her eyeholes glow.

What I like best about her is hard
to explain, but I know the closer I stand

to her body, the less the camera recognizes
me against the blue screen.

INSTRUCTIONS FOR MARRIAGE
BY SERVICE

Surely she's worth seven years,
the black girl who hangs

in the corner like a dress,
insisting on silence

with her rosebud eyes. I drink
from the family cup

solemnly while she dances
a ghost dance with herself.

O fertile is that field and ripe.
I earn my keep by keeping

my head down like a boxer
or an ox. Balanced

on my ladder rung between
those I must obey and she

who hides a tiny spider in her
skirt folds. I earn her

a little each day like
a dropper full of wine. Let her

damned sister dance in green
stockings. Let funerals follow

us like dogs on the road.
And let her be worthy

of the sweat I'll spill over her
for years to come.

BY JOVE

I was in one room looking through a camera.
She was in the other room, unaware
I was looking at her through a camera.
The woman I wanted to hold
my genius thoughts in her belly
like a deep pain from some past assault
forgets me and forgets me.
So I become my race's curator
of inconsequence, seeing the world this way
down through the clouds that blot out
Olympus. The mortals perform
hard labor for my enjoyment, comely
animals I might imitate if the mood
strikes, and the little towns
are all at war. Living means changing
till we're painted on a vase. Then
no one notices when the gods die. Even if
I were still loved it would be
like one loves the unbridgeable
distance of an ancestor, or the anonymous
author of a common recipe. Manhood
is not manhood which buckles
under history. But if I could collect
the stamps of her nakedness
I might arrange them into a bright peach
blossom to hide my animal face.

OUR FURRY FRIENDS

Slaves we coddle in the kitchen.
Collar and stroke into loving
our way, the clang of a silver
knife across the plate. We love your secret
colors displayed through plastic,
separation of bone from flesh,
familiar shade of blood rising up
from the fat. It's all so easy:
the best parts fall right off into our laps.
Since you are harmless,
you must not suffer like we do
when our skirts are raised to our waists.
O to peel back your skin and wear
your innocence out on a Saturday night!
Our fluffy rumps and wobbling
heels almost suffice. So happily
we digest each thrust and slice to be
nearer to you, whose blank eyes
flutter like checkbook pages.

THE PERFORMANCE

It's not right that she should do this
to her body as she speaks,

but it's the only way we can understand her.
We who weren't raised on sand

and cherry pits. Whose stepfathers
held their tempers.

The South is a mean place
we forget about. The windows

boarded up all over town. She says,
dogs chased her down the tar-

soaked road like devils. Each dog with three
heads, three tails. She says,

we might've mocked her story,
but never now. First, she strikes nails

against her chest like matches.
Then, when we think we can't

take more from her, she eats
her own hands. Who are we now

to say that art should not destroy us?

LETTER FROM A NEW ENGLAND GIRL

You hide me in the cupboard and I stay here
for years in darkness, counting
imaginary toads, sucking at my hair.

What was hunted haunts my body:
the fingernails growing in the mouth

of a whale. The picket fence was built
around my waist to dam the miniature

ocean my organs swim. If I reach out
my little pink fist, the air stings it. So I wait,

swallowing repeatedly my body's
wrong opinion of itself. I remember

me in a chair with lamplight offering up
my shape like a gift to the crowded room.
I remember the adoring looks each time

I stuck myself with pins. Whatever I chose
the women said yes and the men said no, or

the men said yes and the women said no.
To me their judgments tasted
like Christmas. I, who feel that I am blessed

with both beauty and a modest soul, still wonder
what you think sometimes since I'm unable

to see you. I would tell you that I'm still here,
decoding the messages, inflicting

only the right kind of violence.
I'm afraid, lest I should offend, to ask

what would happen if I tore you away from me
like a bandage from an old wound.

CHARMED

When I finally emerge from my rickety
wooden house, the light has already moved on.
This makes my image soft
on the doorstep as I slip my kid gloves
over my fingers one by one.
From here I look down through
the constellations circulating as if in cream.
The wren and nuthatch lift my skirt hem
from the mud and I'm ready
to descend. There is a machine
that delivers me from here to there
with expediency and care. Anything I wish for
it places in my hand miraculously.
Its voice is the voice of one hundred hounds
singing noel, and its arms are the bleeding
arms of trees. I do my shopping
with pleasure, and my hat gives a little nod
to the other hats, and my knees curtsy
to the knees. All the dainties
are whisked away into a linen sack
for later. As evening falls, the streets empty
and windows, like one hundred movie screens,
begin to glow. A young boy follows me
through the lanes at twenty paces, ringing
his bell so I never feel alone.

YOUR SERVER FOR THIS EVENING

I slice a wedge of lime, slitting
the center so it holds to the glass.

I wipe the frost from the lip
of the plate with a cloth,

then touch it to my face, tenderly.
What you ordered was

specific, but you are patient
while I travel to the freezer,

searching out your favorite meal.
You are able to discern

between blue ice and blue-gray
ice with your eyes closed.

I know your habits better than
you know my name and your palate

is the bible from which I learn
my verses. How you cover

your lap with the napkin and
which bones you taste first

from the sugar skeleton,
show me that you are a gentle,

lonely person. No wonder
you pay so handsomely for

my company—you think I need
another reason to adore you.

LAYING THE CLOTH, ET CETERA

Each day you understand a little more
your place here. Your face: a pious
landscape. You listen for the bell's double
ding-a-ling through the hallways
like a call to worship.
Hands fold like napkins. Lips hold
together with a stitch. Gradually, you learn
to starch your collar high
and tight, know the moment before
the moment a guest turns to go, to swing
imperceptibly with the door. What
a long hinge the body makes.
Day and dark depend on preparation,
laying the cloth according to the hem
and fold, the flower basket or family
coat of arms facing always
up the table. After dinner, you dig coal
from your chest with a grapefruit spoon
and your eyes scour twenty
dirty plates. The black herd
of boots return, tracking in the sand
and snow you sweep out hourly. If you keep
this up, someday your soul will be
as handsomely arranged as the pantry.

EMPLOYMENT

The skin slips off the fingers so
easily, and the pain up the legs, and pins
between the foot bones; hours
slip like smoke in the lungs or gleam
sharp like one knife
polished after another. It is a wonder
how the self seems not so
permanent after this, yet it keeps
following the sun in its labor,
proving itself to Master,
Father and Mother. I pull feathers
in the rank steam of the kitchen,
baskets from the field, and hair
from my brush when night comes down,
my vision needling to the task. I offer
myself again in all my aspects
but only partly comprehend
the strangers who pass me
on the pavement, in the midst of some
errand, and do not touch me
or speak to me. How must they earn
their daily money? So careless,
the leaves in a quick river.

BLACKFLY

I followed you, farmer, through the rows
all afternoon. Regarding your planetary
path from brassicas to rhubarb and so on till I
dizzied you with my whirling. I clacked
my teeth for your noticing, and wore a little
apron for the blood, wanting
to be your wifey in the summertime.
I spend my money hovering, your straw-covered
head my sun. Lonely love, a hole
filled daily with coppery wine. I would make
a bedroom of your eye, a parlor in the deep
fold behind your right ear, a kitchen
on your tongue, and a wide yard
where the sweat runs down your spine.
Your bigness turns me on. When the meat
of your hand grazes my behind, I long
to scream my sweet alarm, to drive you into
another frenzy of planting.

POSSIBLE NAMES FOR A COUNTRY HOUSE

Hole to Place your Excellent Heart. Your Definitive
Shape. Reed that Bends the Wind. Wind that
Raises a Vault of Bread. Bread for the Millions.
Your Transparent Center. Your Opaque. Willow,
Willow, Willow. The Swinging Gate. Old Village
Prison. Dust to Dust. Shield with Pentangle and Secret
Virgin Mary. Nightmare of Ancestors. Living
Specter. Everything on the Human Scale. Song for
an Orderly Mind. Woodland Huddle. Cache of Promises.
Acorn Stash. Treasured Chest. Where the Diamond
Was Lost from the Ring. Hungry Attic. One Hundred
Christmases. Someone's Childhood Memory.
Another Perpetually Dying Body. The Sinking
Ship. The Lonely Giant. Weathering Whale. Our
Mother to the Baby. Broken Monument.

AUGUST POSTCARD

The men here are failing and the women
failing to help them. Mother sews

a whole forest to replace the other,
inventing fragile creatures.
Without warning, creditors clean
the accounts. We can't begin to repay each other.

The frog's eye follows from a pond of silk
at evening. Pillow for a perching
stone. Above the trees is pillow and she
from her window,
hair pooling on pillow,

leans on it while for nearly a week now
lightning pierces the rumpled field.
Night and day.

MY DEAREST DOLL

My voice like a tadpole finds
the tiny kernel in his skull.

(To fertilize is to be eaten by.)

Before bedtime I tidy
his wooden face. It doesn't move but
I see that he approves.

(Over years I've learned to read
into his aspect a variety of moods.)

He won't remember anything,
overlooks his shiny shoes.

With one eye open I keep
him still after midnight.

Only the black fingers typing
their twiggy nightmares on the glass
will speak to me.

Yet, he is the basket I bury
my eggs in.

REMEMBERING YOUR YOUNG LOVE

First Snow found a corner
to lie down in. Pulled the covers over.
If his/her heart gets buried
under the awning, you know
a hard winter.

First Snow found the underground
hideout. So still, your lover-
worry burns. Low
contrast between dead and living,
a tenuous contract you signed.

First Snow finds you lonelier
than before. Whites out your
calendar, unholds your cold index
finger. He/she consumes you like
water, his/her first food.

If you meet First Snow
on the fairway his/her body dissolves
into the waves around your vessel.
He/she will live with you forever
the moment before.

3

GAIKOTSU

Numerous paths lead up from the foothills,
But behold, a single moon above the peak.

—*Ikkyū Sōjun*

When flesh hangs too heavy
on my foundations and its dirty wounds
weight the words that grow in the air
between us, I wish for the hush of a razor
to shave us both to bone. Our perfect
skeletons would dry up then, and we'd pile
our organs into wicker baskets:
under bare trees burying two slick
livers, yarns of pink intestines, four
exhaled lungs. We could pretend,
while placing my blue-bird womb
in that grave of dirt and blood, that it had
not already died in grief, that its absence
does not somehow bring me fuller.
But pretending then, would be no use.

With the frames of our bodies feeling
each breeze, our iliac crests
would be two pairs of boats toppled
toward each other by masts of spine.
Our smooth scapulae would resemble
nascent wings. When we finished laying
down the dregs of our senses,
we would turn to task, emptying our home
of its insides. Pine chairs, thick woolen
blankets, yellowing books, and
unseasoned bathing suits would clutter
the dark lawn. In echoing rooms
then, we could converse in silence:

one white moon nodding to its reflection
in the undisturbed surface of a lake.

LOVE POEM

I can see where you live but only
through a veil. I let you take care of me so

you will feel close to all the little details
necessary for me to grow.

But you have daily appointments
with the wide world. Like a practical child,

you desire then lose patience with
my adoration, holding me at the length

of an outstretched wing. How will I keep you
if this is the loudest I can sing?

KIDS THESE DAYS

Compared to our ancestors who
sold bread or plowed thanklessly the fields
or hauled fish from the vast seas in nets
they mended in their free time, we have little,
if any, regard for changes in weather.
We are rewarded or punished according
to our behavior, but are safe from God,
who, we've been told, is remote from us,
having left behind other authorities.
At some point today it started raining
very hard and there was no shelter.
We all scattered from the schoolyard
in fifty directions, wearing books on our heads.
There are so many ways to go wrong
that we've stopped sorting them.
The globe is on its stand in the dusty room,
not spinning or teaching anyone a lesson.
There must be a good reason that the whole
world seems so anxious on our behalf.

TENDING THE FLOCKS (ENGLAND, 1790)

> Contagion was a vague concept. It was something—a force
> or body—that transferred disease or caused its transfer into
> a living entity. That force or body might itself be living or
> dead, or perhaps a bit of both.

—*D. T. Max*

Of course from the outside, I couldn't see
the holes in their brains. Just the stiff,
lopsided way they held their heads,
their enormous appetite for sex
(each one fucking many times a day),
and in the last stage, the furious
itch at the base of the spine they couldn't
relieve, turning their creamy wool
bloody. It was, I dare say,
difficult to see my flock in agony
this way. Their gentle, shallow eyes
now angry, mechanical. I thought:
All my unborn children will be devils.
It seemed an omen about family, or man's
folly, that I couldn't quite discern,
but what good is an illegible message?
The idle winter came on again, harvest in,
and the bodies kept falling in exhausted
quakes to the cold grass. In this season
I watched my labors fail, my small
power taken. If, in His wisdom, He revealed
just one greedy secret to myself,
I might believe His goodness. But I am
no use to God nor victims
of possession and disease nor art, and
I never made one penny from those sheep.

PRION

In contrast to all other known infectious agents,
which are living (viral or bacterial), the prion is
a protein, nonliving matter in a misfolded form.

Like a dance, the new shape
caught on quickly. One body
touched another, and the other fell
in line. Surprising, how easy
to reform what our maker forms
in us: press against a spine
just so, and it turns to imitation.
This new shape loved
to see its world as mirror,
but was also a lover of secrets.
It desired—or, because it couldn't
quite desire, demanded—
its own face invisibly everywhere.
It worked its magic so patiently
years passed before anyone noticed
the change: black, empty
rooms growing up out of matter.
Meanwhile, the shape was making
a vast army of itself,
its members indistinguishable
from that one, original soldier.

DON'T

The thread drew a little *x*
to hold the button so

I wear my clothes wherever I go.

There is hatching in the lighter
and darker shadow,

kisses to end the note,
and ribbons up the back that tie me in.

I cross my heart and hope
the eyes of the dead weren't taken,

their starry faces multiplying in the churchyard
like swaths of snow.

For this I walk each morning
the railroad's tired path below black

winter branches

with laces tightly knotted
like chromosomes.

THE BEST BONES

Scotland was an even colder place
back in 1964 if you can believe it. Factories
closed their doors one by one so the men
holed up in the pubs. We lived in a falling down
house where the radio played faraway
bomb speculations. After the stairs rotted through
and became too dangerous, my family
stayed below, leaving in my control
the upper floors. That's how it was
in those days—easy to ignore
the structures sagging over your head.
My parents kept the garden tidy as a kind
of make believe. Sister, who always had
the sharpest memory, set out a dish of milk
for me at night. I grew white. Years
went by and birds across the window.
I heard that oil was found off the coast.
The country was moving again
though I could not, and so remained
quiet in my dusty sheets like furniture
in a grand residence, waiting for its season.
Finally, after what seemed like a long
time, I forgot my loneliness.

HOME

The little blonde girl won't speak
to the boy. She's carrying on

the ancient squabble about
whose parents planted the Tree of Life.

Nothing I can say will make
the two of them turn toward each other

and resume their game of love making.
What a hard jaw she has! But the boy

will keep trying to bring her around.
Maybe I should call them in for dinner,

but they're at their most beautiful now—
stubborn, with blue light on their faces.

Now the boy is punishing the tree
by shredding up leaves, tossing them

into the creek in handfuls. He had begun
collecting fireflies in his hat

but was afraid of crushing them.
He will wait and see if she comes over,

sits beside him and gives him
her hand. But she is in the darkest shade

humming loud enough for him to hear
while she sweeps and sweeps

the dirt with a branch.
Other dead and broken branches

compose the crust of the earth.
If I could warn them now

before my birth, could I keep
the two of them smoldering here as they are,

she with her quiet fury
and he with his dream of money?

PAJAMAS

There is some protection
a bed can't provide, though
the dirty snow cover

soaks and holds you. Part
is the dark figure who reeked
of cinnamon, faking a clean mouth.

During what happened
night after night,
there half of me prayed
awake inside you like a blip,
a cloudberry.

There's still fear in the bed

but hush, I am *your* mother now.
Bare your milkteeth
for me to brush; unbraid
your cornsilk tail.

Here is the story the pajama pants
tell: Little red horses
rear their heads and hooves,
and hearts alternate
between them on the cream flannel
fully formed. They pulse across

this gap in the pattern.
They pulse across one thousand

arctic miles. You can see the hearts
at once but they are
separate, untouched.

OPHELIA

> In dreams, a writing tablet signifies a woman, since it receives
> the imprint of all kinds of letters.
>
> —*Artemidorus*

I resisted the story so long and thus
believed, unconsciously, its opposite—

a mirror of what I hated, which was
no better, you see. Flesh and hair

so ghostly you could read the veins.
I dredged the pond till my joints

gave my bones away. Just a few
sticks composed in the muck,

sheltering a school of fish. Now,
I thought, at least I can be useful.

If you have a voice, don't
waste it on opinions. Let the evening

audience find you each time as if
by chance. First, a swath of matted

hair, and then the rest: a foal
propped up and hesitant.

THE ARTIST'S BOY

The sofa rises like a horse
from its side in the yellow room.
Wood smoke and ink saturate the air,
obscuring, dividing shape
from shape. One could fade
into the scenery near the glow
of his floating hair, this
perfect baby. Somewhere,
rain slicks up Main Street,
and a man bicycles home
in a navy coat, pushing his hat
into the gray. His whiskers are
damp as a dog's. Flowers tornado
to pavement as he whirs past—
coming from, going to,
a certain place. The child
wishes a room into existence
and it's there. Walls yellow, furniture
warm as a mare. Somehow,
when you see him all nervousness
subsides. Little mouth blowing
on your cheek, those eyes
that seem but painted on his eyes.

THE NEW FAMILY

Clean up the lines to be more pleasing
to the eye. Redefine the faces. Give each a smile.
Meanwhile, the baby is lost from the manger.
Start over from fresh pine. Make the pets
more human, or forget them altogether.
We have moved beyond that old desire
for rough, approximate things. This new way
of thinking lets us add or subtract matter
to modify shape. Yes. We're working
in the real world. Now stand the figures
in a circle and pass them once to the right,
making a gift of each to each. So, with our fingers
distinguished, we can hold each other's
wooden breast to our own like an amulet.

ABOUT THE HAMMER

I've fallen in love with a bear
whose wooden claws aerate the great
fields. Every morning over coffee
I read my dreams from crumpled newsprint
while he lays the hammer on the table.
Across each tool we write the first
three objects it will meet, and our voices
sleep in the telephone cradle. So lucky
he and I: Our home is a small museum
of labor. Inchoate ripples expand
over fields for miles, making
concentric rings. Taking hours
at the shelves to choose from among
the labeled jelly jars, we can no longer
separate words from our work. The sounds
become less and less familiar. This
goes on long into the night: his dark
hair over candlelight, implements lined
on the yellow tablecloth, row upon row.

THE MONASTERY

My hair was not on fire
and the fabric of my shirt
didn't rub me the wrong way.
It was the best day of my life

when I entered the monastery.
My heart was not on fire
but enclosed by a high wall
and covered with new grasses

for the white cow who had
taken up residence there.
Each one of my fingers wished
for exactly the same thing—

to curl around the cold
edges of a dish, spend their long
lives washing bowl after bowl.
I fulfilled their desire

by kneeling in the grass
and taking one bowl down from
the tower at a time. I placed
the clean ones in a row

in the sun. The sun was
on fire and it seemed someone
had taken care to arrange
an exact diorama: My feet

fragile beneath their leather, legs
heavy as pillars, and in my head
the hen whose beak can hold
just one pearl at a time.

CALENDAR

If I wait long enough
between the rusted trees
where young mothers take their sons walking
I know they will
airlift in the crates of books.
There will be Proust and Flaubert,
the Russians, ancient religious texts,
and from Poland a calendar
of gourds. I imagine myself turning over
the pages:

each page a picture, each picture a ripe or carved-out womb
with a lighted candle, each page a month I will burn through.

I envy the boy holding
his mother's hand in the woods.

I have a body made hard by work
in other people's homes.
A curve. A crooked
jaw. Pockets full of moths.
Gray beard. I don't want
children, no, I want to be a child.

If you look for a new house
you must consider
the previous tenants, the price.
My head used to have so much space in it,
a sky with white birds darting
like shooting stars.
Now I'm more like a machine: furniture

bolted to the floor. But
my mother.
           But an old man.
I became an old man so early.

WHEN YOU ARE DEAD

you'll look out from under your blue hood
and listen to the echo

of your family making food,
separated only by night's heavy cover.

You had a lover, but now you're a fish
holding your place in the river. Nothing

catches on your long, smooth sides.

Your sister is saying something
about her day—radio music

vibrating around her
in little waves that look like pebbled glass.

The ocean bubbles passionately. All
slides into it from the cutting board.

Please don't worry about the little things—

When God leans down and stops
your breath with one word,

He retires your body like a beloved coat.

Then you'll see the grass up close, and the ants
who never tire of pushing crumbs around

and share just one thought between them.

BLUE WHALE

Dark body dropping through fearsome space

You are the lump in my ribcage

Whole and stony as the Coliseum

Water so thick so salty it packs you in

Your skin like a rubber dove

Would move under the hand without landing anywhere

All there is is nothing

All our selves without a core continuous

White potato heavy with dirt

It hurts to watch it sinking

In the cold wash bucket

A man swimming with rocks in his pockets

Thinking *down I go*

This life of holy proportion

Moment beginning the roller-coaster dive

The light almost reaching you windowless

An empty house sliding into the gulf at night

Vacated by its lovers

Something you didn't expect poured out of you

But your heart is a stolen carriage

Your veins are avenues

Your face cages your food

Our crime toward you was jealousy

O to be a mansion steering itself

NOTES

"Still Birth" borrows its image of the "eggs with pennies inside" from the artist Kambui Olujimi's installation titled "Great Escape."

"Remarks on the Morning's Work in Winter" and "Laying the Cloth, Et Cetera" take their titles and inspiration from *The House Servant's Directory* by Robert Roberts, which, when published in 1827, was the first book written by an African American to have been published in the United States by a major publisher.

"A Bathing Gown a Girl Can Make" makes use of text from *The Book of Knowledge: The Children's Encyclopedia*, 1911.

"To My Daughter" includes a line from William Blake's poem "The Mental Traveller."

"Instructions for Marriage by Capture" and "Instructions for Marriage by Service" were inspired by Ethel Lucy Urlin's *A Short History of Marriage: Marriage Rites, Customs, and Folklore in Many Countries and All Ages*, 1913.

"Gaikotsu" means "skeletons" in Japanese. The epigraph for this poem is from a work of the same title by Ikkyū Sōjun (1394–1481), a Japanese Zen Buddhist monk and poet.

"Tending the Flocks (England, 1790)" has an epigraph from D. T. Max's wonderful book *The Family That Couldn't Sleep*, which explores the phenomenon of prion diseases and humankind's relationship to and understanding of these diseases through history. The poem "Prion" was also inspired by this book.

"Ophelia" has an epigraph from Artemidorus of Daldis, a professional diviner who lived in the second century. He is known for a five-volume work on dream interpretation, the *Oneirocritica*. I first found the quotation in Marina Warner's book *Monuments and Maidens: The Allegory of the Female Form*.

ACKNOWLEDGMENTS

Many thanks to the editors of the following journals, anthologies, and websites where these poems first appeared, some in slightly different forms:

32 Poems: "Your Server for This Evening"; *American Literary Review:* "Please Listen to Us" (now "Kids These Days") and "Blackfly"; *Best New Poets 2011:* "Don't"; *Bone Bouquet Journal:* "August Postcard"; *Cincinnati Review:* "Body Exhumation" (now "Exhumation"); *Collagist:* "Blue Whale" and "Temporary River"; *Drunken Boat:* "The Artist's Boy," "Calendar," "Charmed," "Fable," "Instructions for Marriage by Service," "Ophelia," and "Remarks on the Morning's Work in Winter"; *Harvard Review:* "Wallflower"; *Hollins Critic:* "My Dearest Doll"; *Iowa Review:* "1917" and "Prion"; *La Petite Zine:* "About the Hammer" and "Possible Names for a Country House"; *Literary Review (TLR):* "The Performance" and "Mary"; *Lumina:* "The Lord Is Risen Indeed"; *Memorious:* "Laying the Cloth, Et Cetera"; *Mid-American Review:* "Carving the New Family" (now "The New Family") and "When You Are Dead"; *Natural Bridge:* "To My Daughter"; *Pleiades:* "Tending the Flocks (England, 1790)"; *Ploughshares:* "The Monastery"; *Poetry Northwest Online:* "Letter from a New England Girl"; *Provincetown Arts Magazine:* "Still Birth"; *Quarterly West:* "Sisters"; *Greensboro Review:* "The Only House in the Neighborhood"; *Terminus:* "Gaikotsu."

Thank you to the editors of *Verse Daily* for featuring "The Performance," and thanks to *Mid-American Review* and Mary Biddinger for honoring "When You Are Dead" with the James Wright Poetry Award.

I would like to thank my many teachers and mentors for their support and generosity, especially Stuart Dischell, Linda Gregg, Kevin Pilkington, Ann Lauinger, Joseph Lauinger, Stephen

Dobyns, Tom Sleigh, David Rivard, Vicki Posey, Randall Lathan, and Dennis Hagerman. I would also like to thank my talented peers who have offered camaraderie and invaluable feedback on my work over the years, especially Tony Aarts, Christina Duhig, Stephanie Rogers, Josh Exoo, Michael Morse, Erica Ehrenberg, Courtney Dillon, Joellen Craft, Lauren Moseley, and Tasha Golden. For their brilliant and caring advice on drafts of this manuscript, I am indebted to Michael Peterson, Stuart Dischell, Alan Shapiro, Maurice Manning, Deborah Bernhardt, Joshua Weiner, Ross White, and Brian Brodeur. I am also grateful to Kathleen Kelley and Jasmine Irvin for being my soul friends and allowing me to accompany them through their deeply inspiring lives.

Several wonderful institutions and programs have helped to support me in the writing of this book through generous fellowships and scholarships. These include: the University of North Carolina at Greensboro, the Fine Arts Work Center in Provincetown (with special thanks to Salvatore Scibona), the Bread Loaf Writers Conference, the Weymouth Center for the Arts, and the Virginia Center for the Creative Arts.

I would like to thank Ed Ochester for selecting *Best Bones* for the Agnes Lynch Starrett Poetry Award and everyone at the University of Pittsburgh Press for giving my work such careful attention. It is an honor and a dream come true to count myself among the Pitt Poetry Series authors.

Most of all, I thank my family—Carl, Marie, Brita, and Krista Anne—for their unconditional love and support. There aren't enough poems in the world to express my love and gratitude for you.